This Activity
Book Belongs To:

A Picture of Me

me

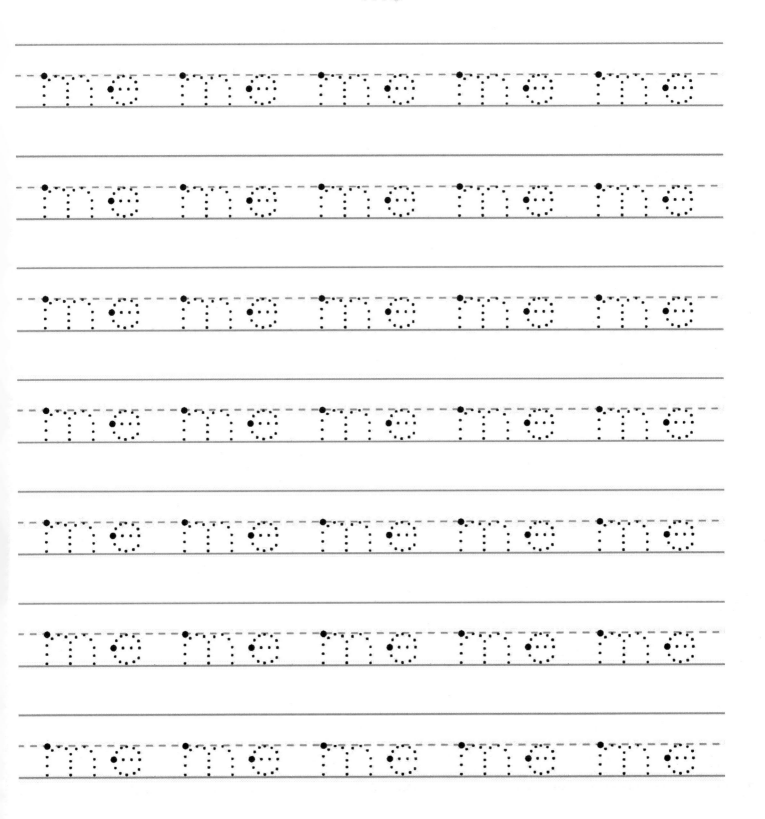

Match the Animal to the Food It Eats

Draw **One** Of Something

Trace the Words and Numbers

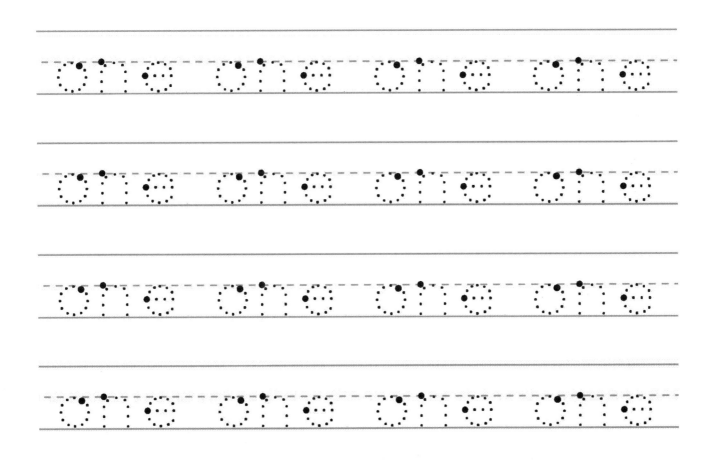

1

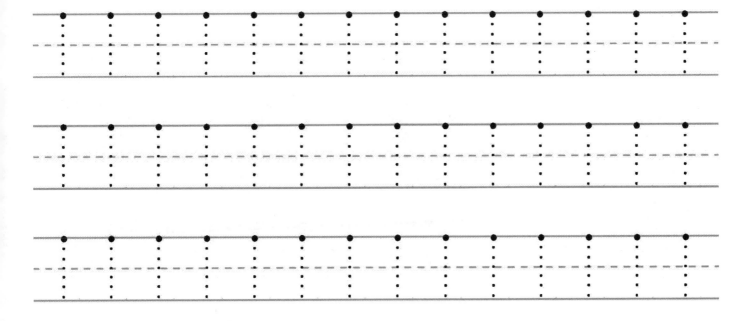

Match the Shadow

Draw Your Family

family

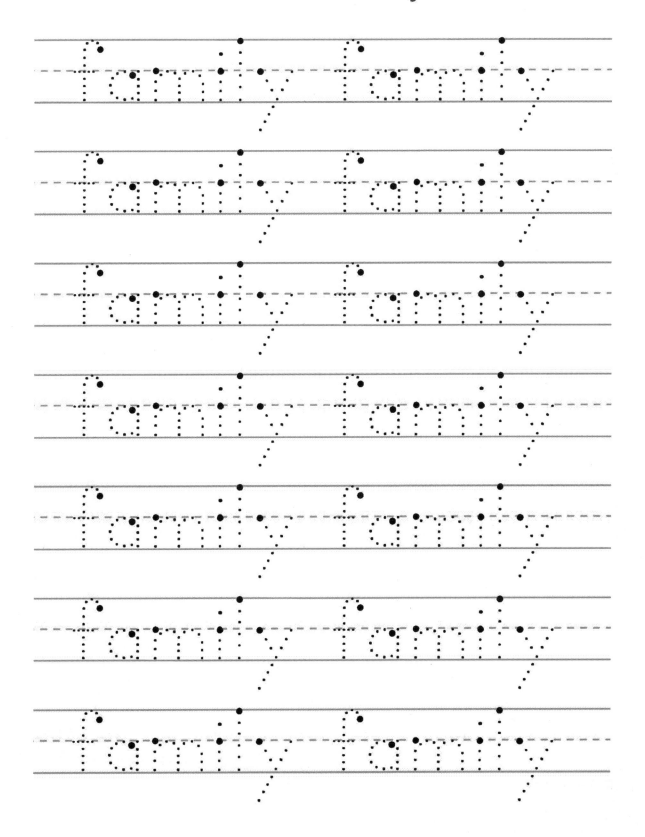

Circle 10 Differences

Which One Doesn't Belong?

Draw Two of Something

two

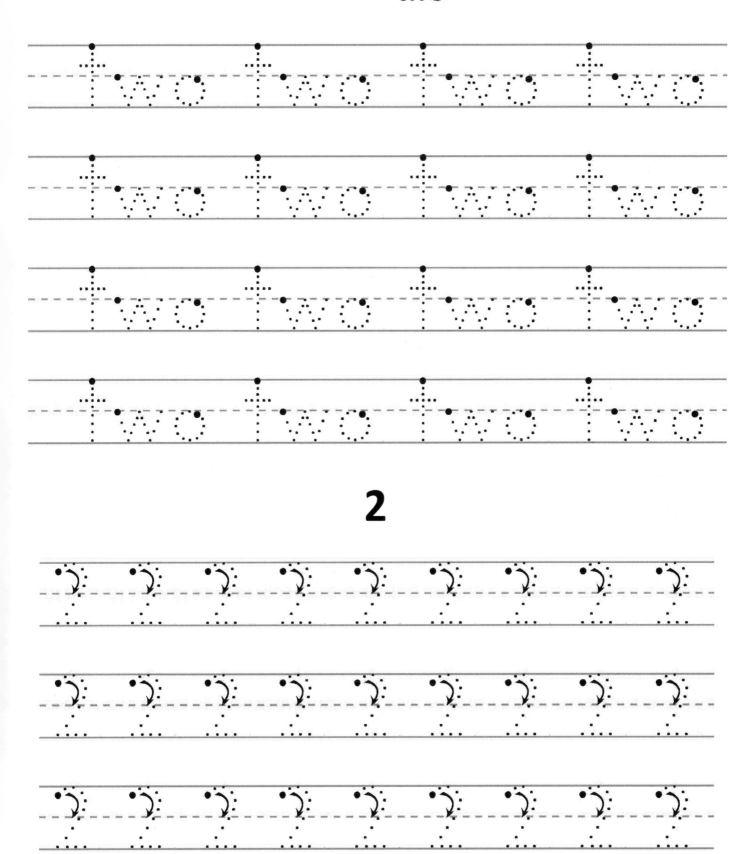

2

Connect the Dots to Draw A Pig

HOW MANY LEGS?

COUNT
&
CALCULATE

(?) + (?) + (?) + (?) = (?)

Draw 3 of Something

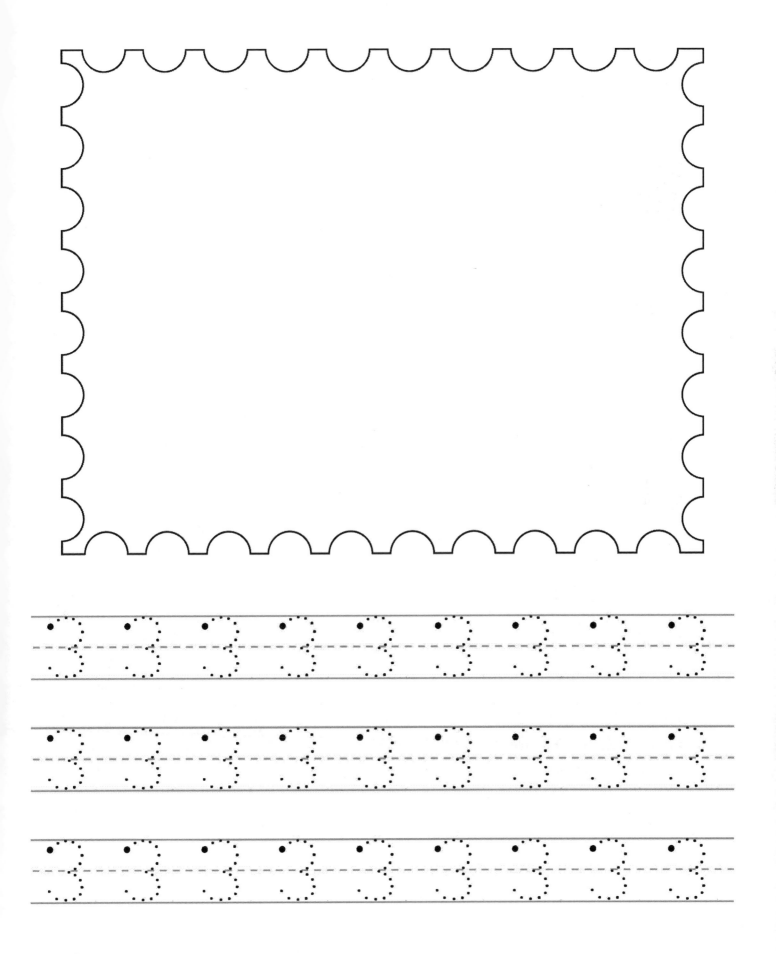

Find 10 Differences in These Two Pictures

Connect the Dots

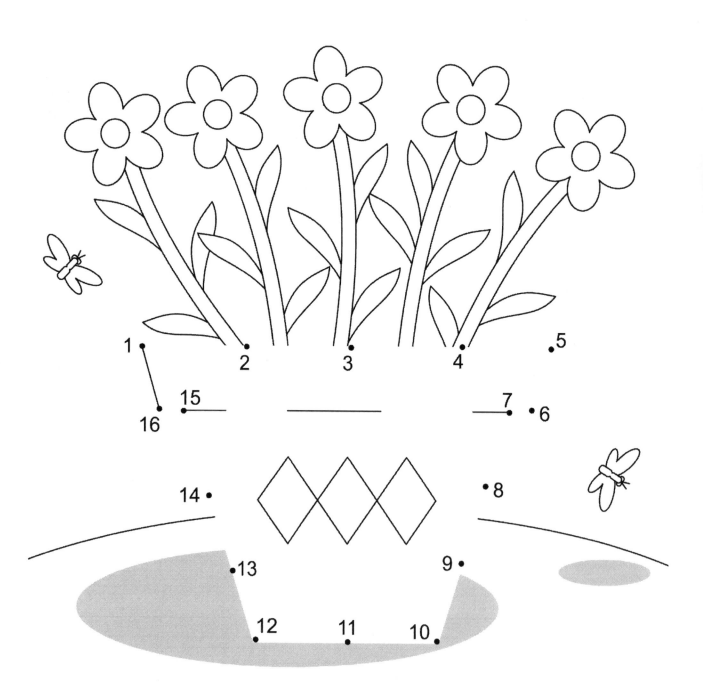

Color the Picture

Connect the Dots to Complete the Picture

FIND TWO
THE SAME
PICTURES

Which One Doesn't Belong?

Find 5 Differences

Find the Matching Shadow

How Many?

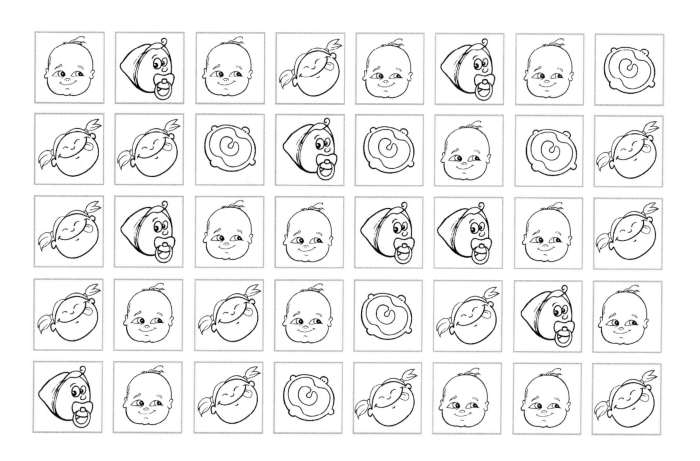

Circle the Objects That Starts with Each Letter

E...

K...

O...

F...

HOW MANY LEGS?

COUNT & CALCULATE

(?) + (?) + (?) + (?) = (?)

FIND
ONE
OF A KIND

Draw 9 of Something Here

Trace the Words and Numbers

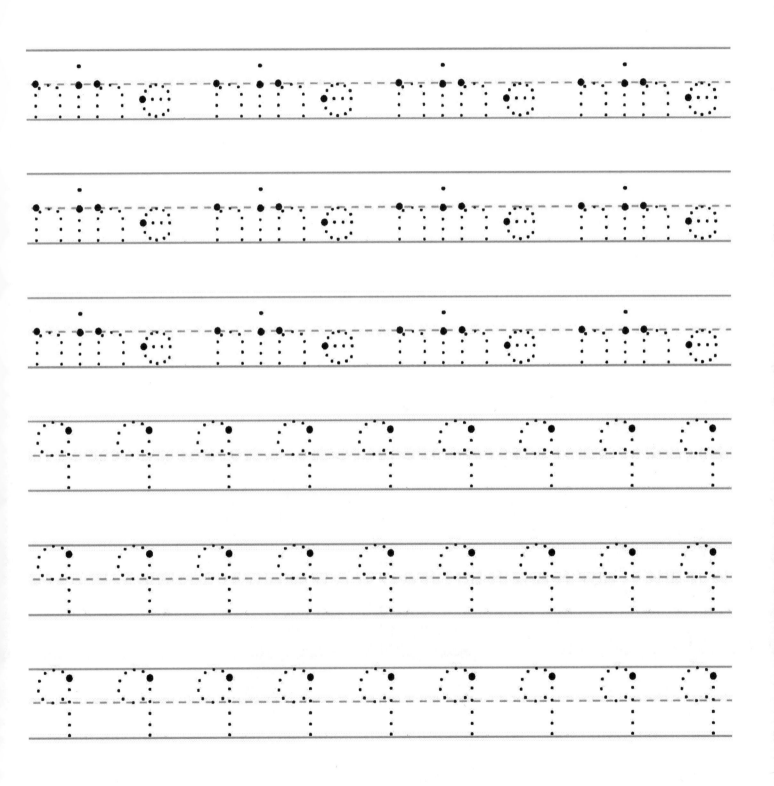

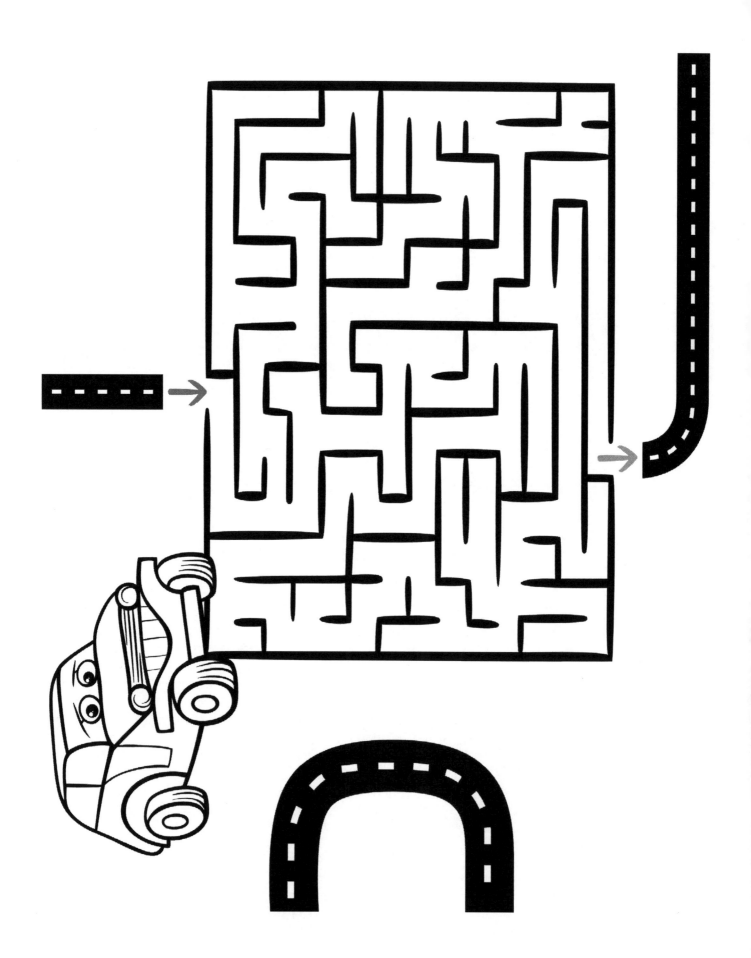

Draw Your Favorite Pet Here

Trace the Word

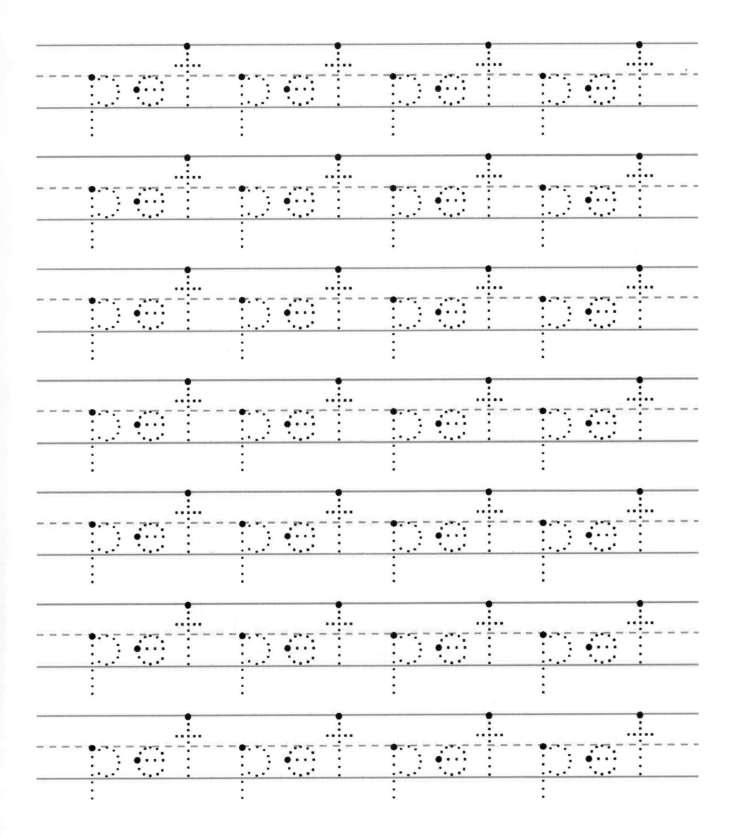

Find 6 Differences

Follow the Steps to Draw a Fish

Draw Your Fish Here

Follow the Steps to Draw a Turtle

Draw Your Turtle Here

Draw 1 of Something Here

Trace the Words and Numbers

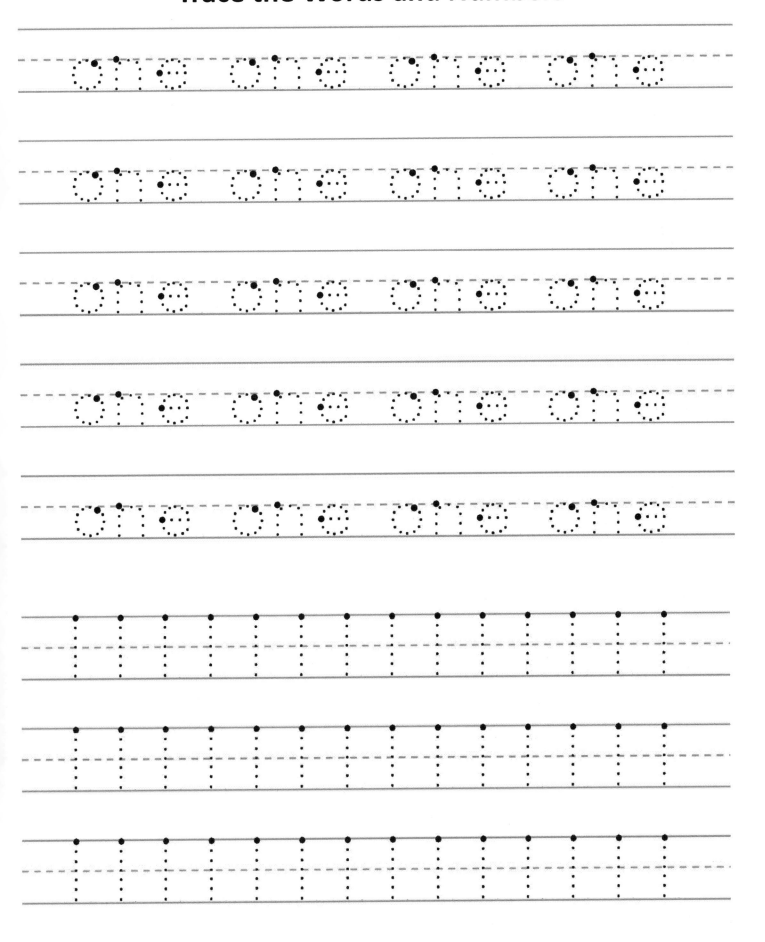

Follow the Steps to Draw an Ice Cream Cone

Draw Your Ice Cream Cone Here

Draw 4 of Something Here

Trace the Words and Numbers

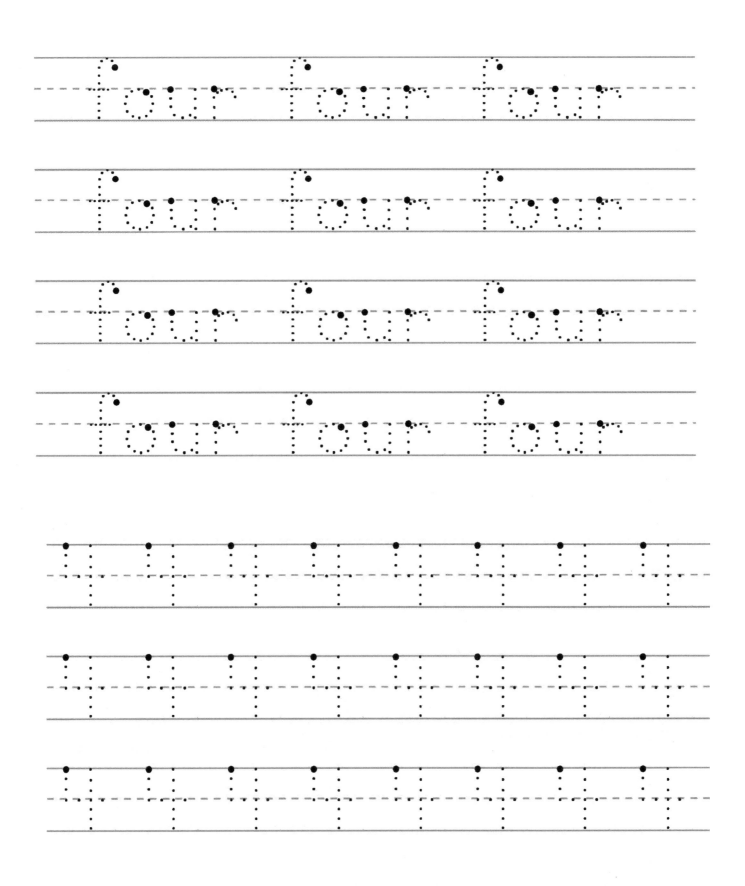

Draw 5 of Something Here

Trace the Words and Numbers

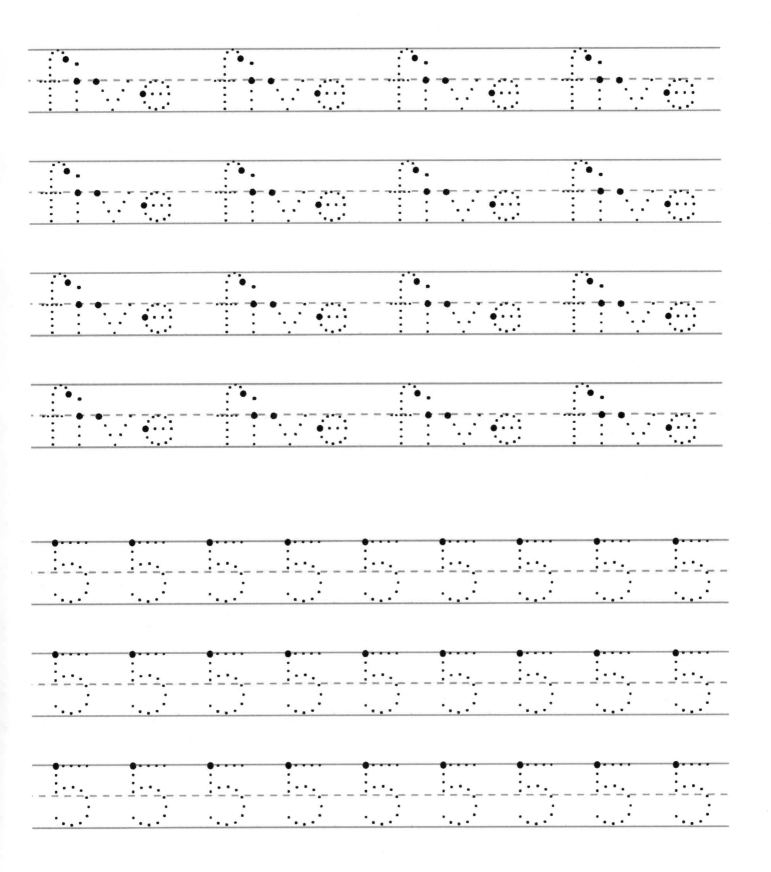

Trace the Words and Numbers

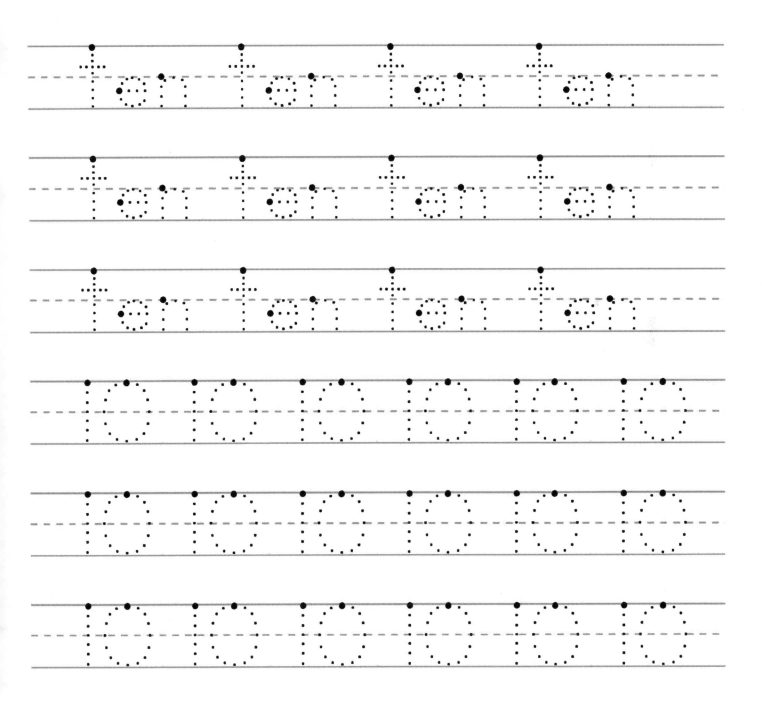

Draw 10 of Something Here

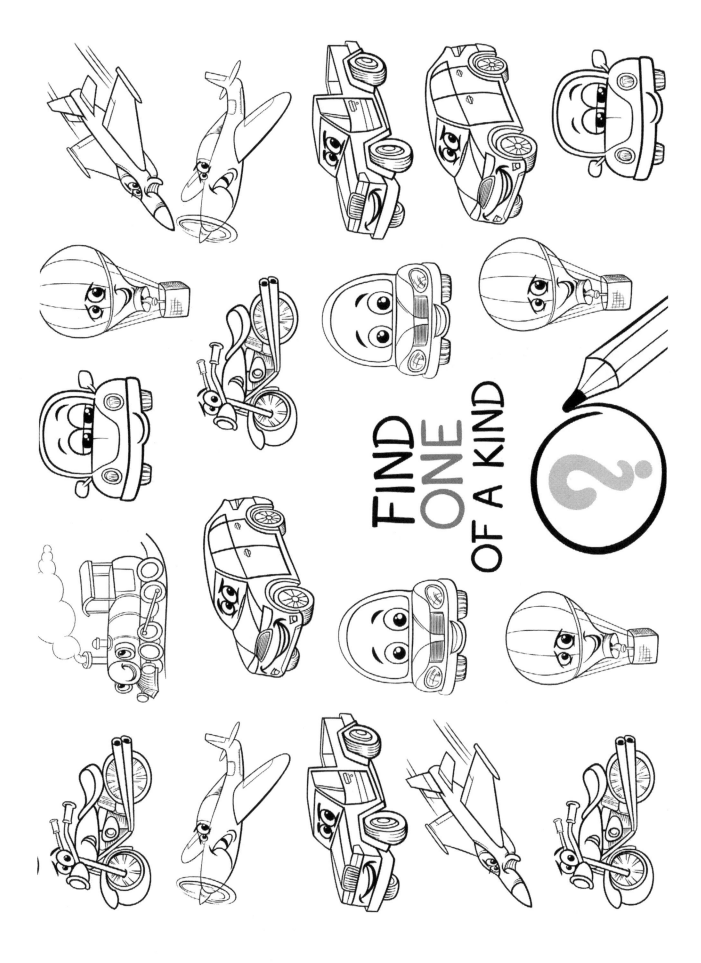

FIND
ONE
OF A KIND

Which One Doesn't Belong?

Find the Matching Shadow

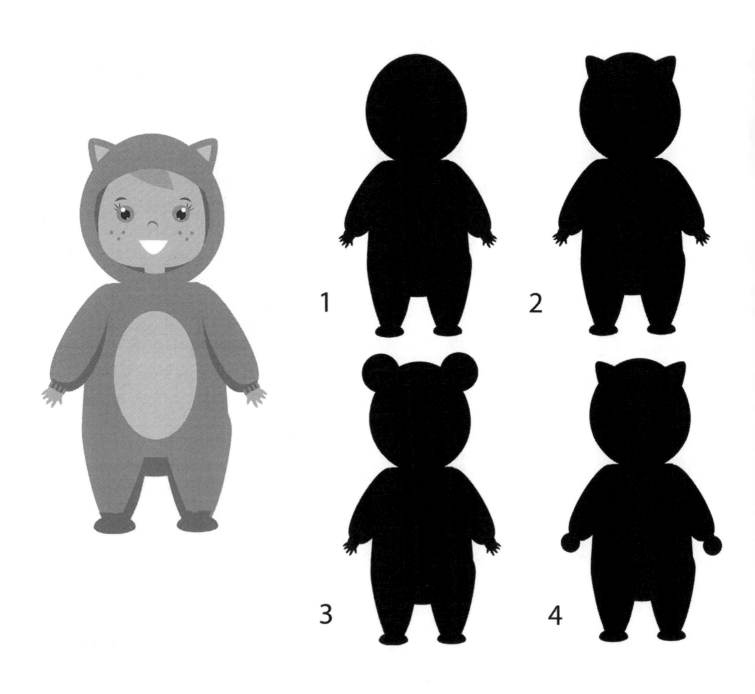

Trace the Word

cat cat cat cat

cat cat cat cat

cat cat cat cat

cat cat cat cat

cat cat cat cat

cat cat cat cat

cat cat cat cat

Draw a Cat Here

Draw 7 of Something Here

Trace the Words and Numbers

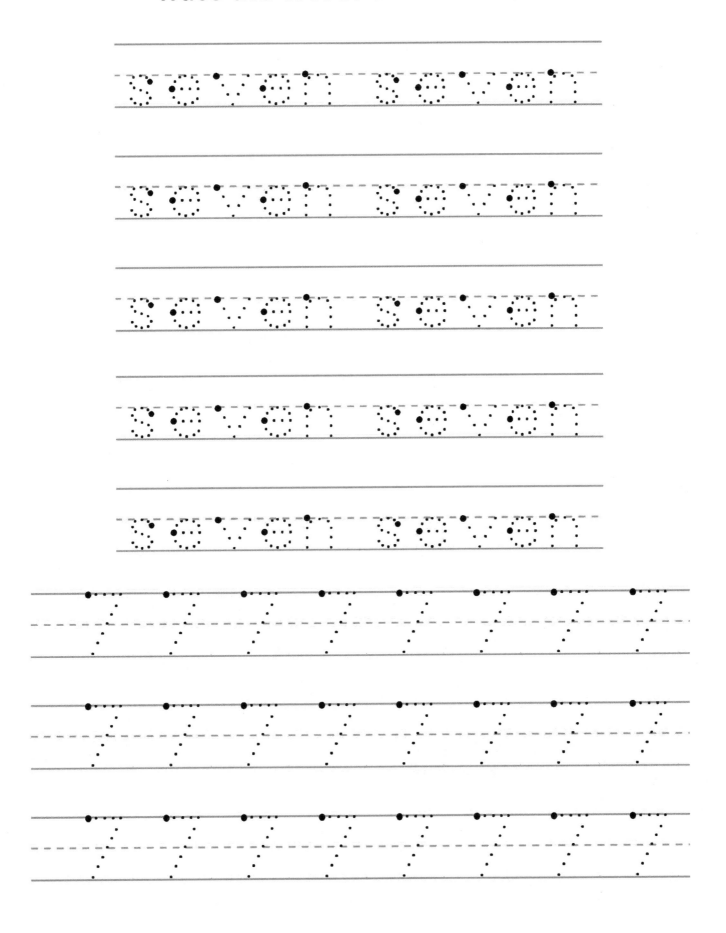

Draw 8 of Something Here

Trace the Words and Numbers

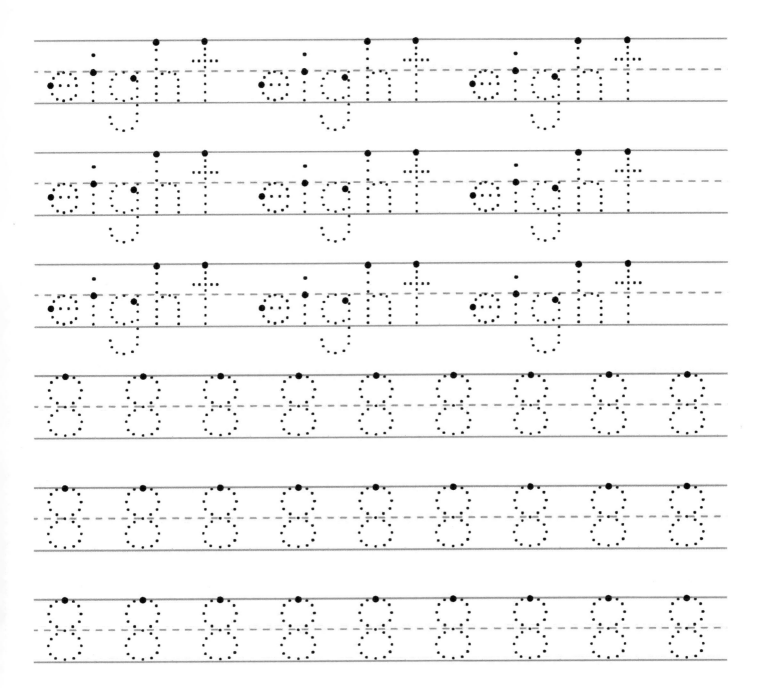

Circle the Objects That Starts with Each Letter

G...

J...

S...

H...

Draw a Dog Here

Trace the Word

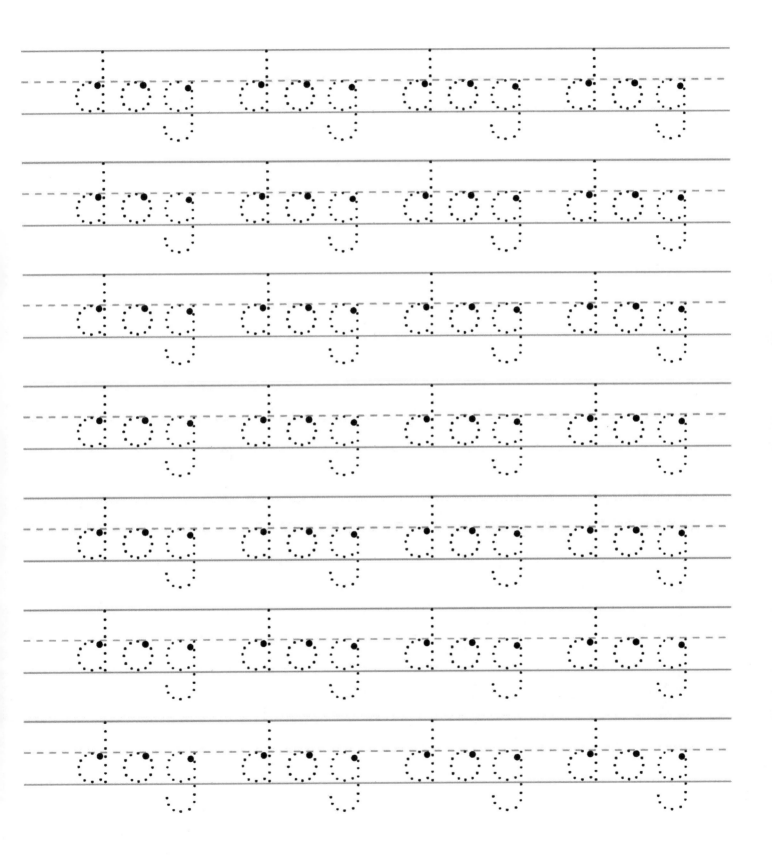

Find the Matching Shadow

Help the Motorcycle Get Home

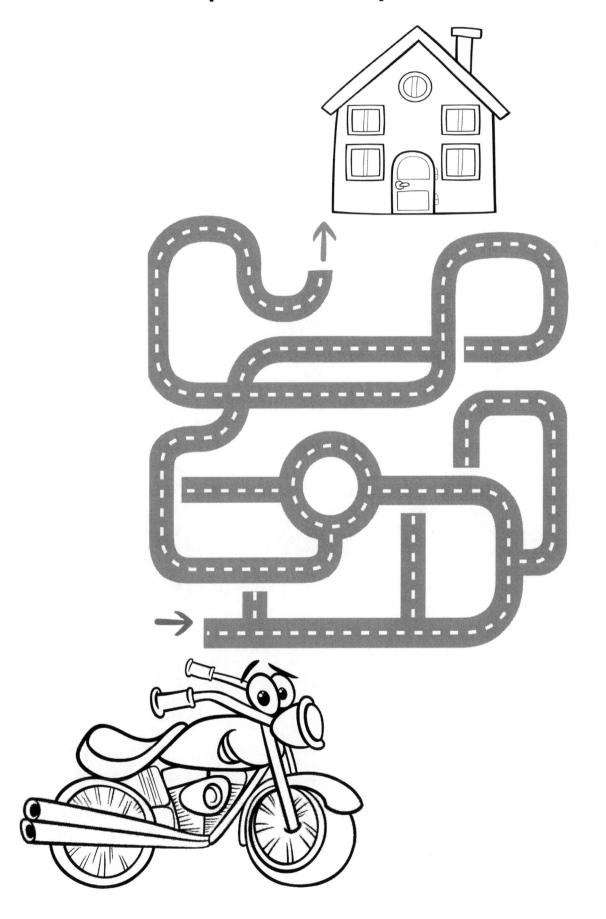

Match the Animals to Their Name

BAT

HARE

HORSE

WOLF

SHEEP

FOX

Write the Letters in the Correct Box to Form the Word

R-2   I-1   A-5
T-3   B-4   B-6

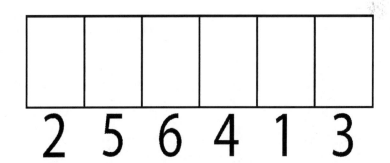

2　5　6　4　1　3

Spelling Word Scramble

Use the letters to spell the word.

E T G

I R

CRAYONS

Trace the Letters

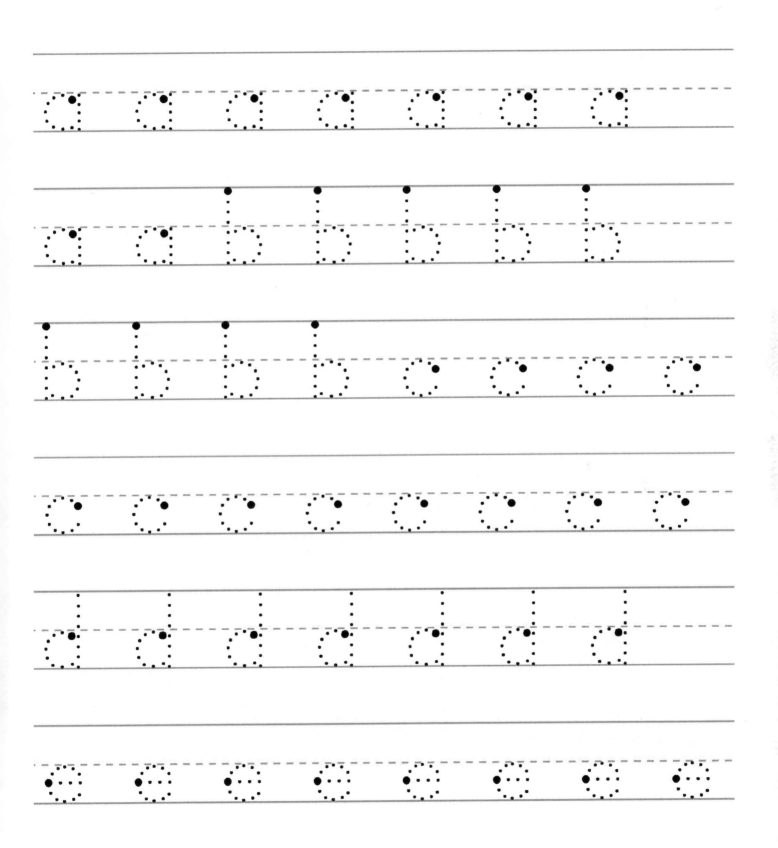

Trace the Letters

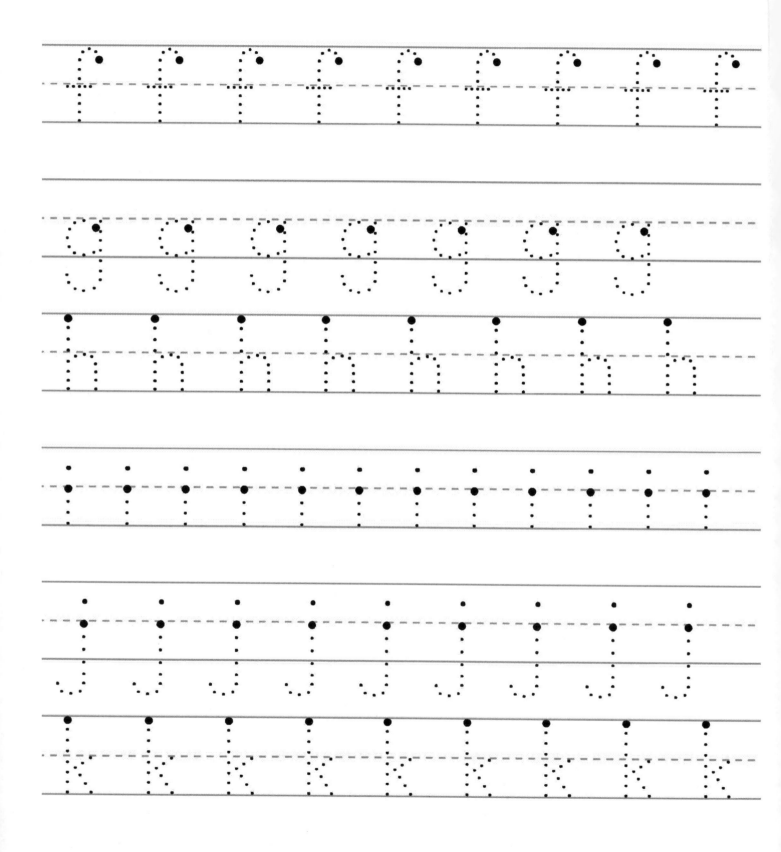

Trace the Letters

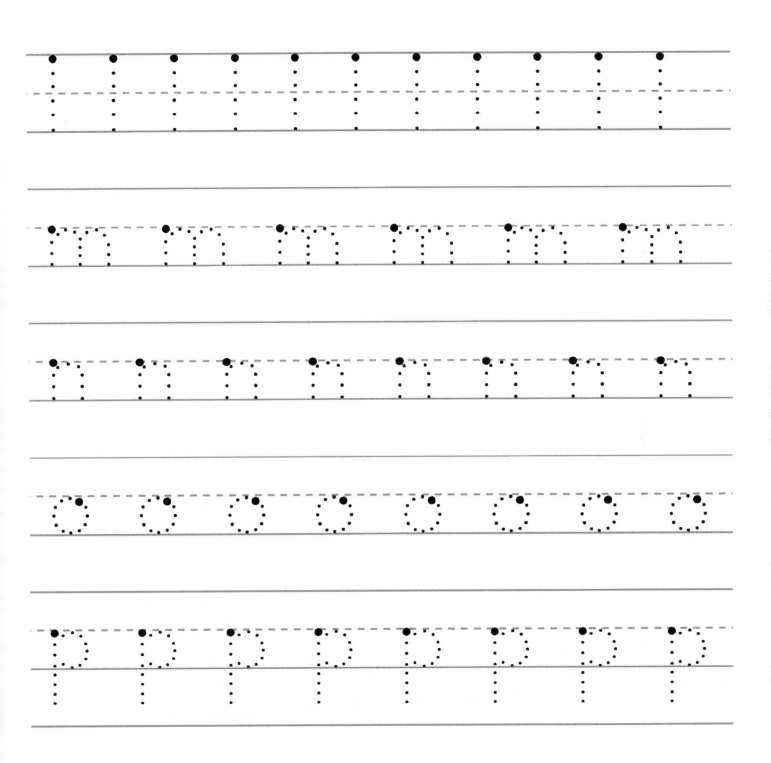

Trace the Letters

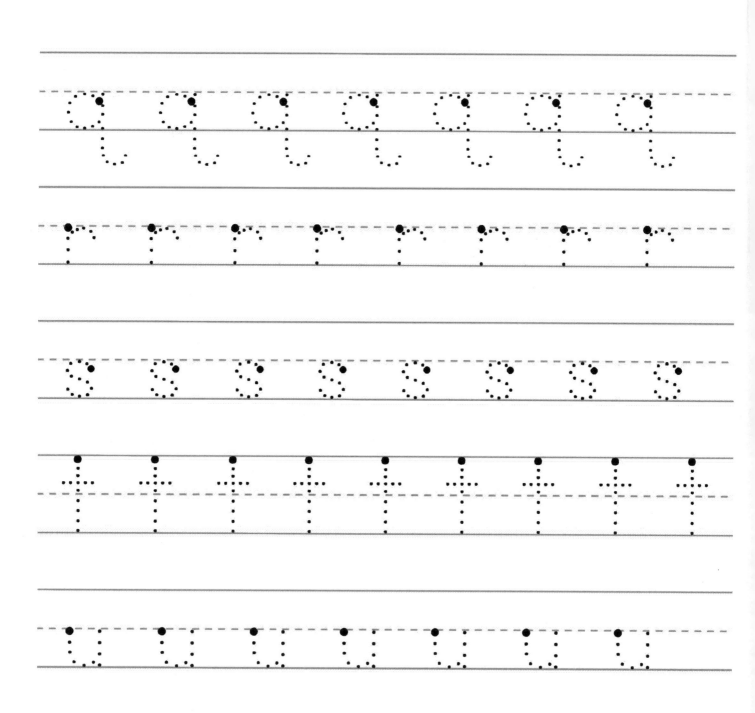

Trace the Letters

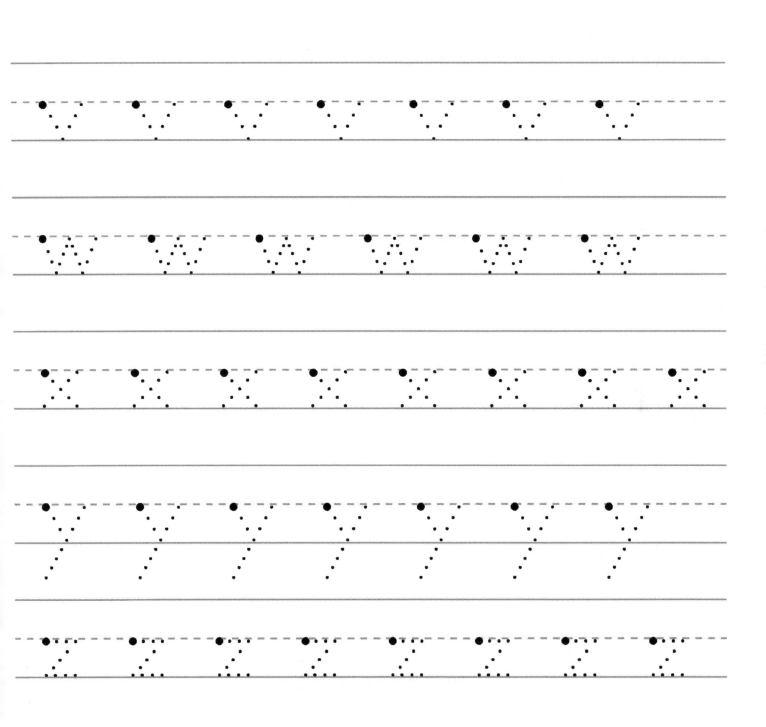

Trace the Letters

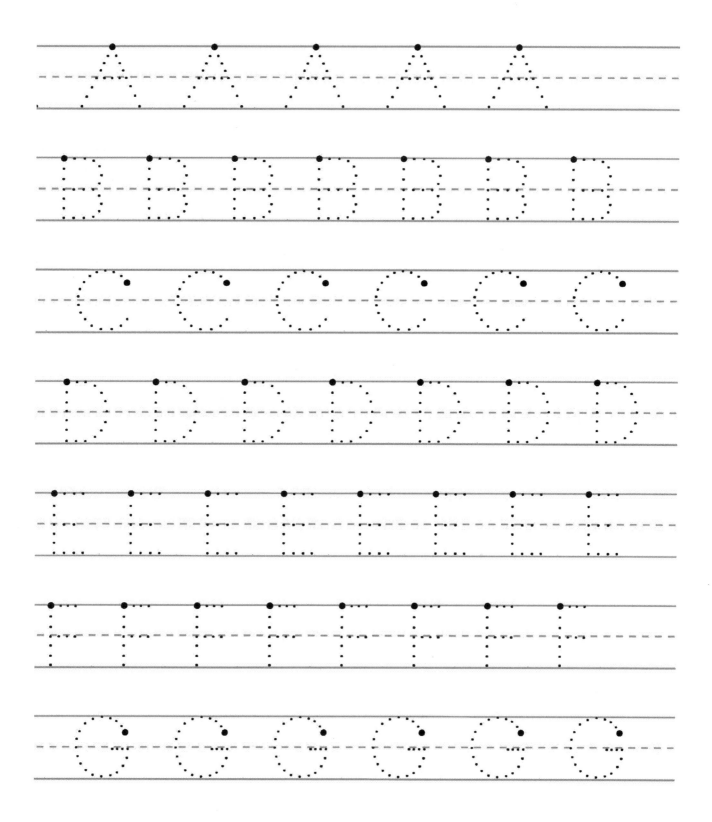

Trace the Letters

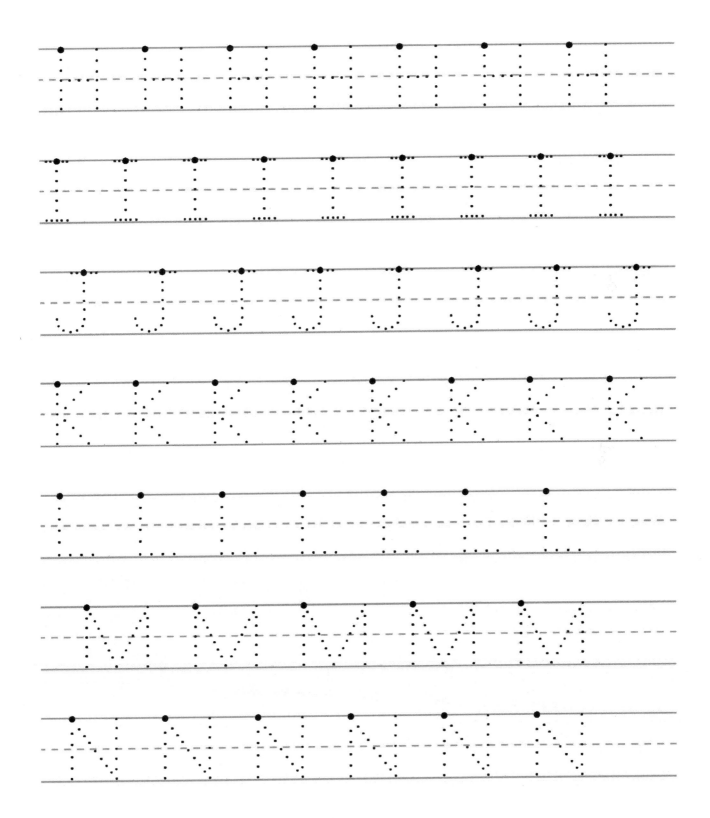

Trace the Letters

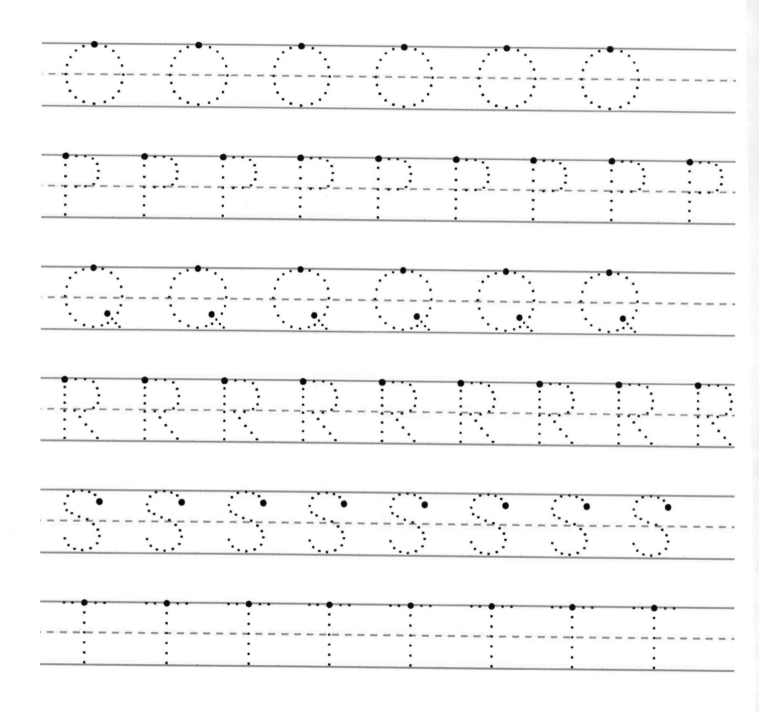

Trace the Letters

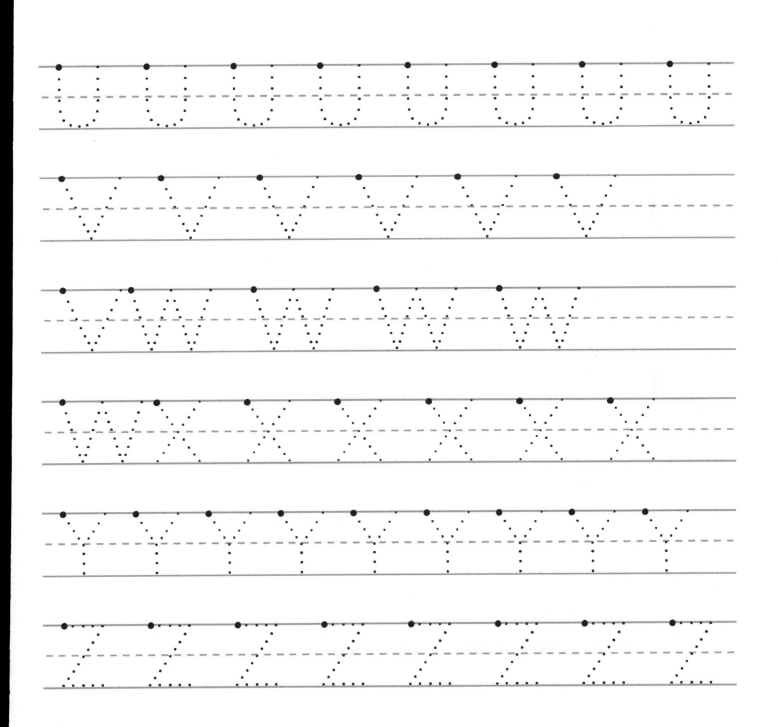

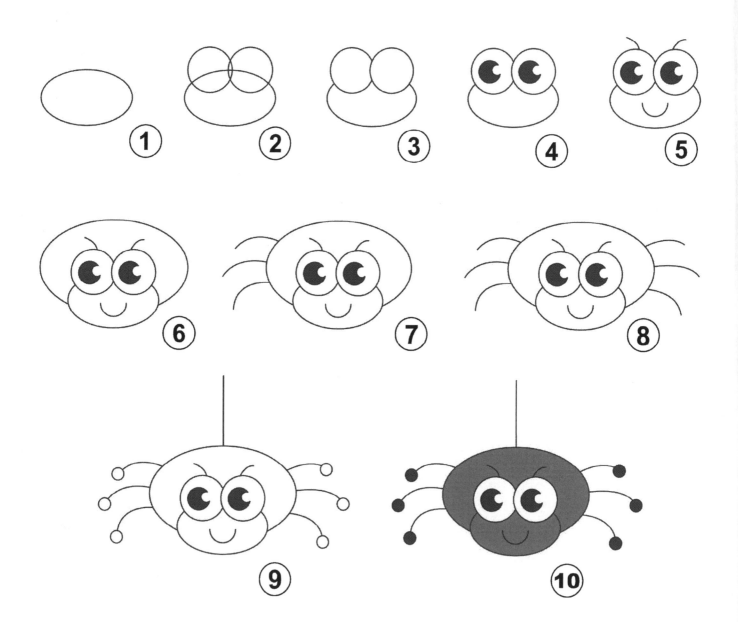

Draw Your Spider Here

Doodle or Draw

Doodle or Draw

Doodle or Draw

Doodle or Draw

Manufactured by Amazon.ca
Bolton, ON

11575155R00061